RHYTHM OF LIFE

WRITTEN BY

COLIN BOYNTON

ISBN: 978-0-9559931-3-8

© 2014 COLIN BOYNTON. All rights reserved.

INDEX

1. COUNTRY LANES
2. TEA GARDEN
3. AT COCK'S CROW
4. THE VISITOR
5. A GOOD LESSON LEARNT
6. UNTITLED
7. INSOMNIA
8. WEATHERMAN
9. RECIPE (TO RELIEVE BOREDOM)
10. SMILE
11. TEMPUS FUGIT
12. THE LAST MAN STANDING
13. INSOMNIA 2
14. THE PHONE CALL
15. STOP!
16. TRUE FRIENDS
17. BEFORE WE SAY GOODBYE
18. MINE FOREVER
19. REMEMBER THEM WITH PRIDE – PAST
20. REMEMBER THEM WITH PRIDE – PRESENT
21. REMEMBER THEM WITH PRIDE – FUTURE
22. WHAT TO DO TODAY?
23. JUST LIKE
24. HOME
25. INSOMNIA 3

26. MY SPECIAL PICTURE ALBUM
27. UNREVEALED
28. THE TRUTH
29. NIGHT TIME
30. TOO LATE
31. TERRORISM
32. SIMPLE & PRETTY
33. I'LL BE HOME FOR CHRISTMAS
34. WASN'T IT FUN
35. I REMEMBER YESTERDAY
36. LOVING YOU – ALWAYS & FOREVER
37. FOR MY VALENTINE
38. DOWN & OUT
39. GROWN OLD
40. THAT'S WHAT FRIENDS ARE FOR
41. PAPER ROUND
42. A WINTER JOURNEY
43. IT!
44. HELPLESS SITUATION
45. WHEN I...
46. SOMEWHERE
47. PASSERS BY
48. THERE'S NO BUSINESS LIKE SNOW BUSINESS
49. DOES IT MATTER?
50. MEMORY MAKERS

51. TWO INTO THREE
52. SITTING
53. WHO?
54. FROM A. TO B.
55. A PLANK OF WOOD
56. BUTTERFLY BREEZE
57. I REMEMBER...
58. AND FINALLY...
59. CHANGES
60. WHAT I LIKE
61. GOODNIGHT & GOODBYE
62. I WONDER
63. NEIGHBOURS & FRIENDS
64. PUT TO SHAME
65. WALKIES BERTIE
66. DREAMS
67. ANSWER ME THAT
68. PRAY SILENCE FOR THE TOAST
69. HEREOS
70. JUST THE SAME?
71. HOPES & DREAMS
72. BEFORE, GOODBYE
73. AN OLD HAT & AN OVERCOAT
74. HAPPY TOO?
75. MISTAKEN IDENTITY

1. COUNTRY LANES.

Narrow, twisting country lanes
Leading who knows where?
Shading branches leaning over
A time to stop and stare.
Views to take your breath away
Hidden by a hedge,
A gap revealing what is there
Beyond the roadside edge.
Narrow, twisting country lanes
Hidden in this view,
And every twist now taken
Revealing something new.
Sunlight shining through the trees
Dappled shade and bright,
A meadow brightly coloured
Enhanced within the light.
Narrow twisting country lanes
Up and down steep hill,
Over water, through a dale
Winding on until,
You find a village small and neat
Hidden in the trees
With tidy gardens full of flowers
And lots of buzzing bees.
Narrow, twisting country lanes
Leading who knows where?
With all this peace and quiet
Do you really care?
Keep on moving slowly down
A narrow country lane
And even if you've been before
You'll come back once again.

2. TEA GARDEN

Who's out in the garden
Partaking of their tea?
Scone with jam and lots of cream
Just for you and me.
With every kind of sandwich
To tempt and to delight,
While sitting in the garden
Enjoying sunny light.
Two old people driving out
A family or three
All stopped by to enjoy
A nice afternoon tea.
With little tables all laid out
There's plenty time to rest,
A pot of tea, a cake or two
Homemade, they're the best.

3. AT COCKS CROW.

The cockerel crowed at half past two
Which really seemed quite strange
We haven't got a cockerel
Within our hearing range.
It crowed again at half past three
The wind began to blow,
Coming down north westerly
It felt like it might snow.
It crowed again at half past four
The rain began to fall,
I really started wondering
If it was there at all.
The cockerel crowed at half past five
And outside it was dark
The weather now was horrible
My dog began to bark.
It crowed again at half past six
I'm sure I'm going mad,
I wanted just to go outside
To see what I just had.
It crowed again 'til half past eight
I went outside to see,
But couldn't find a cockerel
So was it only me?
And then I heard the cockerel crow
From somewhere near around,
My weather vane was swinging
So that's what made that sound.

4. THE VISITOR.

The sparkle in her eyes
Tells me she's alive
And very glad to see me once again.
The smile upon her lips
Her graceful finger tips
As she greets me when she sees me once again.
We're of a different age
It doesn't matter at this stage
I'm glad to see her happy once again.
We're not related any way
I just met her out one day
Now I go to see her time and time again.
It costs nothing just to smile
And to stop and chat a while
It's so nice to see her happy once again.

5. A GOOD LESSON LEARNT

"It wasn't me Mum honest"
A cry you'd often hear,
Trying hard to avoid
That clip around the ear!
The smack across the bottom
That caught us unawares
"No supper now for you young man
Now get right up those stairs."
It seems quite strange now looking back
At all the things we'd done,
The discipline then given out
More often done by Mum.
I'm sure it taught me right from wrong
And how I ought to be,
It didn't do me any harm
I'm happy now and free.
"It wasn't me Dad honest
Who did what had been done"
Knowing that accepting guilt
What was bound to come.
But still we got a short sharp clip
Right around the ear,
To let it be a warning
And make it very clear.
He wouldn't accept mischief,
Or doing any bad,
And we didn't really mean
To upset our Mum or Dad.
I love them more than ever
For all the things they've done,
I'm a stronger person now
And yet a gentle man.

6. UNTITLED

You started out with good intentions
Lots of things to see and do
Very soon you're moving forward
Every day brings something new.
Seeing changes all around us
Nothing stays the same
Is this life that we are living
Or maybe just a game?

We seem to play by different rules
Made by me and you
No dice to throw but still move forward
Take a step or two.
Seasons changing all around us
Time is moving fast
This life that we are now all living
Wasn't meant to last.

We do not know where we are going
Where this is leading to
We just keep going forward
Like we're meant to do.
Changes happen all around us
Sometimes much too fast,
But mem'ries linger in our minds
Of many things now past.

7. INSOMNIA.

Night after night I lie awake
Waiting for the day to break,
Tossing and turning through the night
Unable to sleep I'll turn on the light.
It doesn't help to see the clock
And listen to its tick and tock.
Night after night lying awake
Dreading the time that day will break,
For when I rise go down the stair
I fall asleep in a chair.
I really should have stayed in bed
Taking time to rest my head,
But when I lay myself back down
I lie awake and wear a frown.
Night after night just the same
Sleep for me never came,
Lying awake and tossing around
The world outside makes no sound.
I close my eyes count to ten
Then I count the sheep again,
One sheep, two sheep, three sheep, four
Still awake I count some more.
And as I count them passing by
I see the sun rise in the sky,
Too late for me to fall asleep
After counting all those sheep.
What a waste of all that time
I must get up and start by nine,
And now I'm feeling quite worn out
I'm sure I'll sleep tonight – no doubt.

Or will I ?

8. WEATHERMAN.

I took no coat and took no hat
The forcast said hot sun
I walked out in the country
The weekend had now come.
Walking miles from anywhere
My car was far away
That's when I got soaking wet
On that sunny day.
The rain came down so heavy
I had nowhere to go
So once again the weatherman
Didn't seem to know.
I took my coat and wellingtons
My scarf and gloves and hat,
Went out for a gentle walk
Then by the river sat.
Soon the sun was shining
No clouds were in the sky,
My temperature was rising
I took a gentle sigh.
Removed my hat, my scarf and coat
Trying to get cool
So once again the weatherman
Made me look a fool.
Next time that I am going out
I know what I won't do,
Listen to the weatherman
Because he never knew.
He never gets the forcast right
And seems to get it wrong,
So I shall just ignore him,
The next time he comes on.

9. RECIPE (TO RELIEVE BOREDOM).

Take a little pinch of this
A little pinch of that,
Mix it well together
Then after it has sat,
Add a little something moist
Handle it with care
Stir it well, mix it well
And leave it over there,
After leaving for a while
Turn the mixture out,
Add a little gentle heat
Watch it rise about,
Once you know it's ready
Remove it to a tray,
Gather everything you've used
And throw it all away,
Start again tomorrow
When everything is new,
By following this recipe
You've something you can do.

10. SMILE

Put the smile back on your face
Wear a happy grin
Wipe the tears that's in your eyes
And let the sunshine in.
There's always too much sorrow
Plenty of bad news,
Come with me be happy
Put on your dancing shoes.
Wave away your troubles
Send them far away,
Put the smile back on your face
And wear it all the day.
You'll find it is infectious
You'll pass it all around
It costs you nothing just to smile
That's what I have found.

11. TEMPUS FUGIT.

Tempus Fugit's what they say
But far too fast for me,
Just as one day seems to start
The next one's come to be.
The weeks go by so quickly
The months turn into years,
Age creeps quickly on us
Smiles turn into tears,
You cannot halt the progress
Accept what must be done
Enjoy each moment while you can
The best is yet to come,
Time flies, that's what they say
And with it wisdom grows,
And what the future holds for us
No one ever knows.

12. LAST MAN STANDING.

Starting out together
They'd go through thick and thin
Walking down lifes highway
The bravest group of men.
Standing tall together
Facing life as one
Marching down lifes highway
Until their duty's done.
Remembering together
Everything they'd seen
Looking down lifes highway
Remembering what's been.
Remembering together
Friends that they have lost
Walking down lifes highway
Counting up the cost.
Old friends once together
Departing one by one
No longer on lifes highway
Another life's soon gone.
No longer friends together
An old man sits alone
And thinks about lifes highway
And what is left to come.
The last man standing thoughtfully
Remembering the past
Feeling quite alone asks,
"Why am I the last?"

13. INSOMNIA – 2.

I wish you'd stop that snoring
You keep me 'wake each night
The loudest roar you've ever heard
It gives me such a fright.
It starts a quiet rumble
And ends an awful roar
But please one night I'd like to sleep
Just like I did before.
And if you are not snoring
You're tossing all about
The bed will shake quite frightfully
I'm frightened I'll fall out.
I lie awake just waiting
To see what you will do
Fast asleep quite peacefully
I can't believe it's true.
Then just as I begin to sleep
It starts up yet again
The very loudest snoring
The tossing is a pain.
And in the morning you awake
Looking fresh and bright
Me with bags beneath my eyes
My I look a sight.
"Not a good nights rest?" you ask
"Didn't you sleep well?"
I look at you with mouth agape
What was there to tell?

14. THE PHONE CALL.

"Hello, hello, is that you?
I called you yesterday
I left a message for you
But I've nothing much to say,
You never rang my number
And I waited for your call
I had no news to give you
Well nothing much at all.
There's little else to tell you
I'm sure you will agree
So I'll call again tomorrow
Bye for now – it's me."

15. STOP!

Watching the world go passing by
Day after day all the same,
People all moving in one direction
Each with a different aim.
Moving on forward, no time to stop
No time to look around
Rushing through life day by day
Making a different sound.
Going so fast there's no time to think
Or care about what is out there
All by ourselves yet out in a crowd
No time to stop and share.
The world keeps on turning day after day
And time passes too quickly by
Before we have chance to say "Hello."
We have to say "Goodbye."
So as the world goes passing by
Stop for just a while
Take time just to look around
And maybe try a smile.

16. TRUE FRIENDS.

A shoulder to cry on
When you're feeling down
A smile on their face
When you wear a frown.
A listening ear
When you need to talk
Or be right beside you
When you need a walk.
Someone who knows
But not have to ask
Will give you a hand
No matter what task.
There through your troubles
Sorrows and tears
Stood close beside you
Through many long years.
Someone to share
Your laughter, your joy
Who'll never get angry
When you might annoy.
There in your good times
There in the bad
There when you're happy
And there when you're sad.
Someone who'll be there
Right to the end
That's what I call
A real true friend.

17. BEFORE WE SAY GOODBYE.

Let's take another glass of wine
Before we say goodbye
Share a hug, shake my hand
But please try not to cry.
I know that we will meet again
Although I don't know where
And after all that we've been through
We have so much to share.
Memories of some things we've done
Places we've been to
All the things we ever saw
The people that we knew.
And when we meet up once again
In the years to come
We'll once again remember
All that we have done.

18. MINE FOREVER.

Tick, tick, tock
Goes my favourite clock
That hangs upon the wall,
I wind it up
It runs back down
But I don't mind at all.
I love the sound
As the hands sweep round
It's old familiar face,
And keeping time
As days pass by
In the same old place.
It doesn't chime
It just keeps time
Each and every day,
And though it's old
And wearing out
I really have to say,
It may go slow
But all I know
I'll never take it down,
I'll let it tick
Forever more
As long as I'm around.

19. REMEMBER THEM WITH PRIDE – PAST.

Many marched and many fought
And many lost their lives
Leaving children fatherless
And leaving grieving wives,
They fought with strength and bravery
Not knowing what would come
Facing dangers every day
Each and every one.
They fought from trenches cold and wet
Doing all they could
Fighting on the front lines
Dying in the mud,
They took their own lives in their hands
To fight them in the air
Not knowing if they would return
Or if they'd die up there,
Those now forgotten heroes
Their names are carved in stone
Fought to save their country
Died far from their home,
We may not each remember them
But we should not forget
The legacy they died for
Is all around us yet,
Remember those brave warriors
Remember how they died
They died to save our freedom
So, remember them with pride.

20. REMEMBER THEM WITH PRIDE – PRESENT.

I see their faces every day
Names of strangers to me
Someone's father, brother, son
Why does it have to be?
Do they ever feel alone
While fighting far away?
Do they dream of going home
On that bright sad day?
Are we grateful to them
And do we give our thanks?
Soldiers marching on their feet
Or sitting in their tanks.
Life goes on from year to year
Some things never change
Brave young men getting killed
It really seems quite strange.
"It's just my job" they tell us
"One that must be done"
It shouldn't be their job to die
For me or anyone.
I hope they find protection
And safely get back home
Getting thanks and praises
Each and every one.
Remember some will not return
Remember those now maimed
Stories now familiar to us
Faces that are named.
And when the war is over
Guns put to one side,
Remember our brave warriors
Remember them with pride.

21. REMEMBER THEM WITH PRIDE – FUTURE.

The years will march on endlessly
One day we may find peace
But until then we'll fight the wars
That never seem to cease,
And if we find some peace at last
How soon will we forget
The sacrifice our soldiers made
To them we are in debt.
For as I look around today
At those who do not care
I soon begin to realize
How many are out there,
They live their lives quite selfishly
Thinking of just "ME"
They never seem to think about
They way that things could be.
And some time in the future
As I am growing old
How many will remember
The stories we were told,
Will they want to think about
Those who lost their lives
And think about their families
Their children and their wives,
We never should forget them
No matter when they died
They sacrificed their lives for us
Remember them with pride.

22. WHAT TO DO TODAY?

Here I sit with pen in hand
Not sure what to write
Thoughts drift in and out my head
I just admire the sight.
Should it be quite funny
Or something very sad?
Something seen on TV
Experience I've had?
Do I want to make you think
About the world today?
Or take you to another time
Or place that's far away?
I could just sit and reminisce
Of how life used to be
Way back in my childhood
A happy memory,
When days seemed so much brighter
Summers lasted long
Things that were familiar to us
Now are too long gone,
A world that seemed more innocent
And had a certain charm
When everyone seemed friendlier
And no one caused you harm,
Pictures came in black and white
Sounds in mono too
And life seemed much more simple
The less that people knew,
Perhaps I should just make you think
About the world today
Of how we seem to rush about
Going on our way.

WHAT TO DO TODAY? – CONT.

Where life that once was precious
And treated with respect
Now has little value
What can we expect?
We seem to turn a blind eye
To what is going on
Yet deep inside we're angry
And want to right the wrong,
But still we do not speak out
And say what's on our mind
What are we afraid of
Something we might find?
Perhaps I should just write about
Some far off unknown land
Take your mind away awhile
Make it big and grand,
Fill it full of monsters
A magic spell or two
A princess and a hero
And love that's sweet and true,
A place where every ending
Makes you want to cheer
A place where good beats evil
Each day, every year,
So should I try and make you laugh
Or shed a tear or two?
Make you feel excited
Or leave you feeling blue?
I'm really having trouble
Knowing what to write
So, I think I'll put my pen down
And try again tonight!

23. JUST LIKE.

Like two silent ships
That pass in the night
Like moths that are fluttering
All round a light,
Like seconds that tick
So quickly by
Like snowflakes that drift
So slow from the sky,
Life could be lived
At a more gentle pace
Instead of the speed
Like life is a race.

24. HOME.

It doesn't matter what I do
With friends or all alone
It seems no matter where I am
I want to get back home,
And there is only one place
I hold dear in my heart
I'll always make my way there
To be not long apart,
I know that I am fortunate
Wherever I may roam
However long it takes me
I'll find my way back home.

Home where I find comfort
Home where I find rest
Home where I feel safe
Home is always best
Home for my tomorrows
Home that holds my past
Home for me this moment
Home again at last.

I know that when I get there
I will not be alone
There's someone waiting for me
For when I get back home

HOME.

25. INSOMNIA – 3.

Tossing and turning
I lay awake
Wishing and hoping
For day to break
What is the point
Of lying in bed?
Wide awake
With thoughts in my head
Thoughts going round
Of what I could do
Keeping me 'wake
All the night through
And worrying that
When morning arrives
I'll finally find
That sleep hits my eyes
But too late to sleep
Too late to rest
The day's going to be
One, long test.
Wishing and hoping
When night comes around
I'll lay in my bed
And sleep safe and sound.

26. MY SPECIAL PICTURE ALBUM.

I have a picture album
That I hold dear in my heart
And I always have it with me
Whenever we're apart,
It's full of smiling faces
People that I know
And slowly year by year
I watch my album grow,
Some pictures now are fading
They've been there for so long
And turning to the front
One or two have gone,
Lost and gone forever
Or faded out of view
And as my album ages
These pictures will grow too,
But as my album ages
I'll put new pictures in
Of people I hold dear to me
Since like I did begin,
I wish that you could see it
But it's mine and mine alone
You cannot hold it in your hands
It never can be shown,
It's here within my memories
Here deep in my heart
A special picture album
Of loved ones who depart.

27. UNREVEALED.

I thought I must be dreaming
When I drew the curtains wide
I couldn't quite believe my eyes
The view I saw outside,
I pulled my slippers on my feet
And rushed on down the stairs
Two by two I took them
Then passed the hallway chairs,
I ran in to the kitchen
Opened wide the door
The sight I saw before me
Knocked me to the floor,
I looked outside in wonder
Stood out and looked around
Speechless now and awestruck
I couldn't make a sound,
And so I pinched myself to see
Yes I was awake
I took a step more closer
And did a double take,
If I hadn't seen it
With my very eyes
I wouldn't have believed it
And thought it all just lies,
More in shock than wonder
I turned and went inside
I couldn't quite believe myself
No matter how I tried,
I made myself a cup of tea
Sat and stared outdoor
I haven't seen that sight again
I hadn't seen before.

28. THE TRUTH.

Where did you get
What you've got on?
You look an awful sight,
And when I saw you
On the street
I got a dreadful fright.
Who cut your hair
And styled it so?
It really isn't you,
The scarecrow look
Is not in vogue
You know what you should do.
Get a hat
That covers it
But not that one you wear,
On second thoughts
Just buy a wig
To cover up your hair,
You don't look well,
Are you ill?
You've gone a funny hue,
You don't like
What I'm telling you
And I know what I can do,
WELL!!!!

29. NIGHT TIME.

Silence falls so softly
As night time spreads its wings
Light turns into darkness
And hides a thousand things.
Some things best forgotten
Some best left alone,
Others just a memory
Until the night is gone.

30. TOO LATE.

Should we worry,
Should we care?
Just what happens
Right out there,
Can we change things
Will they stop?
Just keep on going
'Til we drop,
Think of me
Don't think of you,
Just one bad thing
That we do,
Faster, faster
On we go,
The pace of life
Does not slow,
No time to falter
Or to pause,
No time to think
About the cause,
Onwards, upwards
Ever on,
Before we know
The day has gone,
Just for once
Can't we wait,
Before it all,
Becomes
TOO LATE!

31. TERRORISM!!!

They seek him here, they seek him there
The mouse that sat beneath the chair,
He scared the lady half to death
She screamed so loud she lost her breath,
She turned bright blue and then passed out
While the mouse just ran about,
It seemed to smile, it seemed to laugh
They should have took a photograph,
Who'd have thought that that small thing
Could terrorise and horror bring,
The more she screamed the more it sat
She wished someone would bring a cat,
Its whiskers twitched it turned around
Then left the room without a sound
And still she screamed and screamed so loud
Outside the house there grew a crowd,
"What's happening?" "What's going on?
Is someone hurt, is something wrong?"
"Get some help" a policeman came
And went inside, much to her shame,
She had to say that all was well
And nothing else would she tell!

32. SIMPLE & PRETTY?

It is simple
It is plain
And some people think a pain
But they tend to pop up
Anywhere they want.
It is small
It is neat
Found in any street
Where people have a garden
Or a lawn.
Is it dull?
Is it pretty?
Found in any town or city
Looked upon by all
Yet passed by many
It is simple
It is plain
And still it will remain
A weed that is a flower
Is the daisy.

33. I'LL BE HOME FOR CHRISTMAS

The road was very quiet
And night was coming on,
The sky was dark and cloudy
Now that day was done,
And still I kept on walking,
A few more miles to go,
The sky became more stormy
And looked like it might snow.
To be here in the country
At this late time of year,
My thoughts began to wander,
But I had nought to fear.

The road was very winding
And seemed to be quite long,
I couldn't quite remember
Had I got it wrong?
For very many years now
I hadn't passed this way,
I felt I should have started out
Much earlier that day.
Memories kept coming back,
Christmases now past,
Now here I was this Christmas
Now come around so fast.

I'd left that village years ago,
A very pleasant one,
But nothing there was left for me,
All I knew was gone
The old folks now had passed away
My friends had all moved on
My family had gone away
Slowly one by one

Cont…

There'd been no need for my return
And so I'd kept away,
But here I was returning
On a cold and wintry day.

I have a lot of memories
One or two are sad
The others make me happy
And make me feel quite glad.

While travelling down upon the train
These thoughts came back to me,
I felt a smile upon my face
That everyone could see.
Would I find the place the same,
Or would I see a change?
Could I ever feel the same
Or would it all seem strange?

I never really missed the place,
Just glad to be away,
But now the journey that I made
Took far too long that day.
I felt the boredom mounting
The journey had been long
Travelling now for many hours
Just going on and on.
The last few miles I had to do
Meant I had to walk
Glad to now be all alone,
I didn't want to talk.

Cont…

I passed the hedges stripped of leaves
And passed some aged trees,
The fields were bare and empty,
I felt a gentle breeze.
The snow began to gently fall
Flakes all glistening bright,
Falling slowly one by one
In the fading light.
I heard the church bells ringing out
Sounding loud and clear,
My step became much easier
As I was drawing near.
I hadn't heard them ringing now
For many years gone by,
I stopped to listen carefully
Then thought I heard a cry.
I shook my head and cleared my mind
Looked out across the view
Nothing much had really changed
And yet – it all looked new.
A mem'ry came in to my mind
Of playing just out there
But that was many years ago
We didn't have a care.

We laughed, we cried and ran about
Oh, what fun we'd had
But now they're all just memories
Making me feel sad.
I thought about the friends I'd known
And wondered where they'd gone
The one's I'd played with in these fields
They too had all moved on.

Cont…

I started walking once again
To leave these thoughts behind
And though they sounded very real
The sounds were in my mind.
The snow was falling heavy now
And laying on the ground
My footsteps fell upon the road
Without a single sound.
Muffled by the snow now
Everything was white
Though darkness now was creeping in
It seemed to be quite right.

I reached the church at half past four
There was no one around
I went in to the churchyard
And never made a sound.
The church was all in darkness
And all so very stil
And soon I found the grave
That's when I felt a chill.
I lay my wreath upon the grave
Said a little prayer,
Turned to look out on the fields
That's when I got a scare,
I felt my heart just skip a beat
I'd thought I was alone
But I'm sure I saw a shadow
And heard somebody groan.

Cont...

I stood quite still and didn't move
Afraid of what was there,
The snow was falling heavy now
And yet I didn't care,
It covered up the tracks I'd made
Not so long ago,
So was there something in the field
And did I want to know?

I took a very careful step
So that I might see
What it was that I'd just heard
And what it just might be.
I took a careful look around
But didn't see a thing
The field was bare and empty
I felt relief begin.

I turned around to walk away
My duty had been done
And thought that next time I came back
Would be in summer sun.

I heard a carol starting
It sounded sweet and clear
I looked across the field so white
The sky was getting clear,
I saw the moon now peeping through
The clouds began to part
That sound of carols from the church
Began to lift my heart.
Many thoughts of Christmas past
Flooded through my mind
And tears that welled up in my eyes
Almost made me blind

Cont…

I listened to the singing
The joy that it could bring
The wish that I could join them
Made me want to sing.

The church seemed all in darkness
Which seemed a little strange
And so I started walking round
And then I saw a change,
A candle started flickering
Almost out of view
The stained glass window hiding it
Behind it's red and blue,
And then it started moving
I heard the singing cease
I thought the service over
Yet, my heart felt ill at ease,
The voices now approaching
Laughing full of glee
I thought I ought to get away
But waited just to see.

The voices got much nearer now
But no one was in sight,
I looked around the corner now
Into the dark of night,
The voices started singing now
Very loud and clear
Some talking to each other
And getting very near,
I felt a shiver down my spine
My fear was rising high
I wanted just to run away
As nothing caught my eye.

Cont…

I turned and started walking
Slowly to the gate,
Wanting now to get away
Before it was too late,
The voices started following
I wish they'd pass me by
But they seemed to be much fainter now
And drifting to the sky,
Soon I was in silence
I turned and looked behind
Were they ghostly voices?
Or were they in my mind?

THE END.

34. WASN'T IT FUN.

Oh the joys of getting old
Creaking joints and feeling cold,
Constant aches and frequent pain
Every day that we get rain,
Can't do this and can't do that
Hair long gone so need a hat,
Legs are shaky knees are weak
Teeth keep slipping when I speak,
The teeth are false not my own
Oh my goodness hear me moan,
Eyesight poor I can't see well
Going deaf but who can tell,
I cannot run can hardly walk
No one hears me when I talk,
And when I'm sleeping all day long
No one wonders what is wrong,
But after all is said and done
I can't complain I've had some fun.

35. I REMEMBER YESTERDAY.
(FOR MAGOULLE).

I remember yesterday
When you made me smile,
As you sat beside me
For the shortest while.
Life is very precious
And passes very fast,
Treasure every moment
Before the moments past.
I remember yesterday
And all the love you spared,
Love with no condition
Was all the love we shared.
Life is very precious
So handle it with care,
Make the most of everything
One day it won't be there.
I remember yesterday
I hope I don't forget,
The joy you brought in to my life
From the day we met.

36. LOVING YOU – ALWAYS AND FOREVER.

We met one night
In quiet light
Our destinies entwined,
You gave to me
What seemed to be
So very hard to find.
I loved you then,
I love you now
I'll love you on and on,
And I will go on loving you
When both our lives have gone.

I found in you
A little thing
And, oh what joy
That it can bring.

I never want to lose you,
I'll never let you go,
Just travel down life's highway
Whilst my love for you I'll show.
You give me lots of pleasure
The little things you do,
The many happy memories
The looking forward too.
Your love is like a treasure
And all the things we do,
As often as we might
Will always seem like new.

We give, we take,
We always make
The best of what we've got
And though it may be little
To me it is a lot.

36. LOVING YOU… (cont)

You give to me,
I take from you,
And in return I give…
…My little heart…
…And all my love.

You make me laugh,
You make me cry,
But tears of joy
Are what fly by,
And time it passes quickly
No bad things come along
We just enjoy a peaceful life
A life that's full of song.

And sometime when we're older
We look back and we find,
That all the things we didn't do
We never seem to mind,
'Cause everything we did,
And all the things we had,
Make up for all the things we missed
And things don't seem too bad.

The living
The loving,
The sharing,
The caring,
Are all a part of our short lives,
Are just some things that make us wise
To all our wants
And all our needs,
The make our lives a little sweet.

36. LOVING YOU…(cont)

And through our lives
We help each other,
Like a Father
Or a brother,
But most of all
You'll always be,
The one that means
The most to me,
My love,
My life,
My everything
Always and forever.

You changed you ways
To suit me,
You do your best
To please,
Our ups and downs
Like merry go rounds
Our ins
Our outs and abouts.

I like the way
You like the things,
That to me
Great pleasure brings.
The countryside,
The seaside,
The trips to nowhere fast,
They all make up the memories
The ones that always last.

36. LOVING YOU…(cont)

Your smiling face
Your warm embrace,
Your words
So sweet and tender,
Your love glows on
Throughout my nights
Just like a burning ember,
It keeps me warm in winter,
And in the mid day sun,
You always seem to have the time
For sharing lots of fun.

And as I lie here dreaming
I always seem to find,
That one important person
Is always on my mind.
You're in my thoughts at waking,
You're in my dreams at night,
You stay with me at noon time
Never far from sight.

I want you always near me
I need you by my side
To always show me what to do
And always be my guide.
I love you now,
I loved you then,
I'll love you through my days,
And I will go on loving you,
Forever
And
Always.

37. FOR MY VALENTINE.

If I could tell the whole world
Just what you mean to me,
I'd talk about your love
And how caring you can be,
I'd talk about the things we've shared
Through good times and through bad,
How you make me smile on days
When I am feeling sad.
The times we've watched the sunset,
Or walked out hand in hand,
Or simply watched the ocean waves
Crash upon the sand,
Whether we are sat at home,
Or on some foreign shore,
Or even many miles apart
I couldn't love you more.

38. DOWN AND OUT.

Walking down a darkened street
Dancing leaves around my feet,
Falling raindrops on my head
I wonder where to make my bed?
Feeling free but all alone
Wishing that I had a home,
Walking parks at dead of night
I keep myself well out of sight,
Moving on a break of day
Afraid of what most people say,
And every day is just the same
For a man who has no name.

39. GROWN OLD.

Grey hair
No teeth,
Wrinkled stockings
Round her feet,
All smiles
Mind long gone,
She walks around
And sings a song,
In a world
That's all her own,
In a home
That's not her home,
Pity those
Who cannot see
Just how happy
She can be.

40. THAT'S WHAT FRIENDS ARE FOR.

A shoulder to cry on
Someone to care
Whenever you need them
You know they'll be there
They won't turn their back
They don't walk away
An ear that will listen
To all that you say.
Someone to laugh with
Someone to care
If they need a shoulder
You will be there
Together in good times
Together through bad
Laugh when you're happy
And cry when you're sad.
The road may be long
And distances great
The day may be early
The night may be late
No matter what happens
Wherever you are
A true friend will always
Never be far.

41. PAPER ROUND.

I'm reading the paper
I bought yesterday
That's full of the stories
And what people say

It's telling of horror
It's telling of joy
Showing us pictures
Of things that annoy

I shouldn't feel anger
I shouldn't feel sad
But the things in the paper
Make me quite mad

I just want to scream
I just want to shout
Make everyone stop
And just look about

Why is there dying
Why is there war
And why is there starving
All this and more

There never is peace
Across the whole world
It's not just the young
It's sometimes the old

41. PAPER ROUND - Cont.

When will we learn
To live and let live
Not bear a grudge
Forget and forgive

I turn the next page
The stories the same
Just different places
And different name

And so it goes on
Day after day
It just never changes
That is the way

Everyone's set
On the path that they take
They will not change now
Just make the mistake

And when it's all over
The headlines should say
"That's all there is folks
The world's had its day!"

42. A WINTER JOURNEY.

In the cold, cold depth of winter
With frost still on the ground
The moonlight spread its silvery beams
And silence fell around,
Nothing stirred the undergrowth
Stillness filled the air
A soft cold breeze whispered by
As if it had no care,
Sweeping through the branches
Of trees devoid of leaves
Then on across the rooftops
To reach beneath the eaves,
Gliding past the windows
Shuttered for the night
Sealing out the cold and dark
Until the morning light,
Inside an old man sitting
Beside a glowing fire
His wife now gently sleeping
The flames leapt high and higher,
Another log brought more sparks
That rose into the flue
Further up the chimney
To disappear from view,
Out in to the cold air
Then slowly fade and die
Hidden by the stars
Up in the winter sky.

43. IT !

Whatever you do don't even move
Don't even make a sound,
Did you see it lying there
Short and fat and round?
It looked at you, it looked at me
I'm sure it looked away,
Whatever it is it looked around
Decided it would stay.
I don't know if it's frightening
Or might it even bite?
I saw one like it yesterday
It stayed there all the night.
Could it be the same one
Or are there more out there?
Should we go right up to it
Do you think we dare?
Should we wait till morning
And see if it's moved on?
We'll come when it is brighter
And hope that it has gone.
So plucking up the courage
We gently crept outside
And still the creature sat there
It didn't try to hide.
We slowly walked up to it
And yet it lay quite still
Perhaps the creature died there
Or maybe it was ill?
We couldn't see it breathing
We couldn't see it's face
It didn't even make a sound
Of life there was no trace
As we stepped up to it
It didn't look so big
And wasn't even scary
It was my Mothers wig!

44. HELPLESS SITUATION.

Another lonely night
By another lonely chair
Lying all alone now
No one else is there,
It's been like that for days now
No one took the place
When her husband passed away
No one could replace,
He'd cared for her for years now
She'd done the same for him
He'd left her all alone there
And still nobody came
As the minutes ticked away
Another day was gone
She knew deep down within her
That something should be done,
She couldn't reach the telephone
She couldn't reach the door
Everything too far away
As she lay on the floor.
She cursed the old worn slippers
She wouldn't throw away
Although her husband begged her
Almost every day.
He lay by the bedroom door
Since he passed away,
She slipped on the kitchen floor
Only yesterday,
She wondered who would find them
As she fell asleep
And said a prayer to heaven
My Lord, my soul to keep.

45. WHEN I…

I wanted to be something big
When I was very small,
Something no one else was,
No worries, cares at all.
I'd be the man I wanted,
Do what I wanted to,
The dreams I had when younger
If only I then knew.
I didn't want to rule the world,
Or be a superstar,
I didn't want to drive a train
Or drive a big fast car.
I didn't want a mansion,
Be wearing fancy clothes,
I wished to lead a simple life
But is that how it goes?
As the years went quickly by
I grew up very fast,
I didn't stop to think about
My dreams from in my past.
I wanted to be something big,
And look at me today,
My tummy growing rapidly
My weight has run away.
Not quite what I had dreamt about,
Or wanted to become,
It's time to do some exercise
And lose my growing tum.

46. SOMEWHERE.

Somewhere in the world
There's always someone crying,
From hunger or from pain
For someone who is dying.
Somewhere in the world
Someone needs some caring,
Someone needs a helping hand
From someone who is sharing.
Somewhere in the world
A new born baby cries,
Helpless in its Mothers arms
Is where the baby lies.
Somewhere in the world
A new born baby dies,
Its Mothers arms are helpless
As she sits and cries.
Somewhere in the world
Someone sits alone,
With no one there to care for them
And no one who will come.
Somewhere in the world
Someone lives nearby,
Do you know that someone
And do you hear their cry?

47. PASSERS BY.

Have you seen the old man
Walking down the street,
Do you wonder where he goes
Or who he goes to meet?
Have you seen the old man
Sitting in the park,
Do you wonder where his thoughts are
Sitting there till dark?
Have you seen the old man
Plastic bag in hand,
Full of precious memories
From simple to the grand?
Have you seen the old man
And asked who he might be,
Where it is he's coming from
Or who he goes to see?
Have you seen the old man
And asked who he once was,
Was he someones husband
Should I ask because,
I haven't seen the old man
He wasn't there today,
And no one seems to know his name
Or care in any way?
I haven't seen the old man
I won't see him no more,
And people keep on passing by
Just like they did before.
They never saw the old man
Yet passed him every day,
Lost in their own little worlds
As they go their way.

48. THERE'S NO BUSINESS LIKE SNOWBUSINESS

It only seems like yesterday
When I was just a boy,
The snow that fell quite heavily
Was always such a joy.
Living in the countryside
There's nothing we could do,
The lanes were blocked, the road was closed
And all we had to do
Was get a bag or get a sledge,
Get out in the snow,
Rushing down the hillside
Watch everybody go.
Fathers, daughters, mothers, sons
Everyone was there,
From morning until night time
No one had a care.
Snowball fights and snowmen,
Getting wet and cold,
No one seemed to worry
From young ones to the old.
And even as the daylight fell
With night time drawing close,
We stayed out in the moonlight
Until we nearly froze.
We finished very cold and wet
Our snow time fun would end,
And then back home we all would trudge
A neighbour and a friend.
And when the daylight came once more
With more snow lying there,
Once more we'd go in to the fields
For fun for all to share.

49. DOES IT MATTER?

If you remember some of the things
That I remember today,
You told a lie about your age
You're older than you say.
It gives it away when we chat
Of things from way back when,
People we knew, things that we had,
Gives it away again.
You said you were born in nineteen hm hm,
I never once believed that,
'Cause if you remember who and when
You'll also remember where at.
Don't deny your memories
You don't look all that old,
Enjoy the past and all we had
And all that we were told.
Age is a number and nothing more
You're only as old as you feel,
Somedays I feel just seventeen
Others as old as the hill!
Your wrinkles give you character,
Your grey hair you can dye,
The aches and pains come easily
And pass nobody by.
Age is a number I've been told
It doesn't bother me,
As long as I am happy,
Be what I want to be.

50. MEMORY MAKERS

Looking through old photographs
Made me stop and think
Where have all the years gone
Vanished in a blink,
Here today, gone tomorrow
Now just a memory,
Of times we spent together,
And how things used to be,
They cannot be recovered
Brought back to life again,
Just lie there in my memory
To bring me joy and pain.
Looking through old photographs
Bring people back to me,
Some of them still with us
Some a memory,
Things we did together
And things we did alone,
Making friends along the way
I wonder where they've gone,
They cannot be recovered
As time moves swiftly on,
And so before we know it
Too many things are gone.
Looking through old photographs
Makes me stop and think,
Thank goodness we have photographs
Captured in a blink,
With us for a lifetime,
The subjects may be gone,
But memories are with us
To last our whole life long.

51. TWO, INTO THREE

With sunshine on the water
And waves upon the shore
Footprints left behind them
Soon gone just like before
A fleeting time and moment
Two people hand in hand
Walking on the seashore
And strolling on the sand
A gentle breeze that's blowing
Out across the shore
With ripples on the water
All this and so much more.

With stars that gently twinkle
Up in the night time sky
Moonlight beams are thrown across
Two people walking by
A fleeting time and moment
Two people so in love
Sitting by the seashore
And never want to move
Arm in arm they sit there
Looking out to sea
And thinking of the future
When two will soon be three.

52. SITTING

Sitting in an armchair
Watching hours go
Sitting by the fireside
The evening passes slow
Sitting all alone now
With no one by her side
Sitting with her memories
There's nowhere she can hide
Sitting with her teardrops
Falling down her face
Sitting with her sorrow
With dignity and grace
Sitting and she's waiting
With nothing else to do
Sitting, waiting, sitting
If only someone knew.

53. WHO?

Who can mend a broken heart
Or catch a falling tear?
Who can heal a memory
Full of pain and fear?
Who can put the smile back
Or bring the laughter out?
Who can soothe the furrowed brow
Bring an end to doubt?
Who can make me happy
Whenever I feel sad?
Who can make me feel good
When everything turns bad?
Who stays there in troubles
When everything goes wrong?
Who is there beside me
When the night is long?
Who is it has patience
And knows just what to do?
Who is always there for me?
No one else but you!

For Frank.

54. FROM A. TO B.

I can't believe the roads today
Traffic can hardly go
And every day it's getting worse
Just moving very slow,
No matter whatever road I take
Whichever way I turn
The traffic soon is standing still
Will I ever learn?
There's road works here and road works there
They never seem to end
And as one seems to finish
There's new ones round the bend.
I cannot get from A to B
Like I used to do
It seems to take forever now
And then the air turns blue,
From people cursing loudly
Frustrated every day,
By all these different road works
Blocking up their way.

55. A PLANK OF WOOD

A piece of rope a plank of wood
An overhanging tree
Nothing more was needed
We had a swing you see,
A set of wheels a plank of wood
A hammer and a nail
Soon we had a go kart
It never seemed to fail,
A few old sacks a plank of wood
An old tree or a bush
Soon we had a makeshift den
It didn't take too much,
Imagine with a plank of wood
All the things we did
Our minds were free and active
When I was a kid,
A piece of rope a plank of wood
Would scare the kids today
They'd feel bemused with what they had
And not know what to say,
They've no imagination
Of what to do at all
A plank of wood ain't plastic
Electrical or small,
It's not run by computer chip,
Doesn't have a screen,
Think of all they miss today
And everything that's been!

56. BUTTERFLY BREEZE

Sweeping across a blue summer sky
On a breeze that is cooling the air
Lightly and daintily coloured so bright
So delicate and so fair
With wings that are fragile and easily broke
Yet able to fly in a breeze
Twisting and turning and flying around
Seemingly with great ease
How many times has one passed you by
Without you seeing it there
Almost touching while flying around
Carried along in the air
How many times have you brushed one away
As it gently touched you with grace
Not knowing what beauty had just fluttered by
On the butterfly breeze on your face.

57. I REMEMBER…

I remember years ago walking down the lane
Laughing in the sunshine time and time again
Searching in the hedgerows, finding a birds nest
Making chains from daisies – whose would be the best?
Everyday was different, finding something new
Boredom never bothered us with lots of things to do.

I remember years ago walking down the lane
Finding shelter under trees while watching falling rain
With water dripping off the leaves
And puddles on the ground
We still had quite a lot of fun splashing all around
The autumn leaves that fell there, also gave us fun
We'd kick our way through them in the fading sun.

I remember years ago walking down the lane
When snow had covered everything
Nothing looked the same
Snowball fights between us, getting soaking wet
Building snowmen by the road
Those times we don't forget
Slipping, sliding, falling down, still we had such fun
Staying outside in the snow until the day was done.

I remember years ago walking down the lane
And now that many years have passed
Nothing is the same
There's no one there to greet me
The hedgerows have all gone
It makes me stop and think about
All that we have done
Everything is different now
And no one feels the same
But I'm glad that I remember
My favourite country lanes.

58. AND FINALLY…

Another voice is crying out
At something else done wrong
And someone sheds another tear
At someone's final song
Another day, another year
And somethings stay the same
A different time a different place
Another hurting game
A different tear a different face
Another kind of pain
A hurt that is familiar
And nothing new to gain
And if we stopped to think about
A way to end all war
A final tear might roll right down
And then would fall no more.

59. CHANGES

So fast the world keeps turning
How quick the changes come
And just as you are starting
Another day is done
You try to keep the pace up
But soon get left behind
And just as you're beginning
There's one more change you find
As fast as you are learning
It's falling in to place
As you start to understand
The world steps up it's pace
The changes keep on coming
And no matter how you try
Just as you are catching up
The changes pass you by.

60. WHAT I LIKE.

I like the smell of new mown hay
I like a setting sun
I like the way a calm descends
When the day is done
I like to hear the blackbirds sing
I like to smell a rose
I like to hear a babbling brook
As it gently flows
I like to see a lamb in spring
I like to hear the bees
I like the sound of gentle winds
Blowing through the trees
I like to hear the silence
I like a country lane
I like to wander down them
Time and time again
I like to be alone now
I like all of these things
I like the joy and pleasure
That nature always brings.

61. GOODNIGHT AND GOODBYE.

As night time slowly spreads its wings
All across the land
The sea just keeps on rolling
Waves upon the sand
And moonlight shines across the bay
Reflected on the sea
Silence creeps across the land
Another day's set free.

62. I WONDER

I heard the sound of voices
But there was no one there
I heard the sound of laughter
Drifting on the air
I felt a chill creep up my spine
The night was still and warm
I thought I felt a gentle touch
Placed upon my arm
I turned and thought I caught a glimpse
Of someone standing near
I felt my body tremble
Was it cold or fear?
I wasn't sure just what was there
Or what it just might be
I wondered could it be a ghost
Or Angel guarding me?

63. NEIGHBOURS & FRIENDS

What became of neighbours
Friends who lived next door
Someone to rely upon
Who never asked for more
Whenever you had need of them
You knew that they were there
Never in each others ways
But someone who would care.
Someone you could turn to
In good times or in bad
Someone you could talk to
Would give you all they had.
What became of neighbours
Who lived there once before
You always looked out for them
An ever open door
If ever they had troubles
You helped the best you could
You always lent a helping hand
In bad times or in good
There for one another
If the need was there
Sometimes you never saw them
But you knew just were they where.
A friend you could rely upon
But never in the way
But there for one another
Any night or day.

64. PUT TO SHAME

Due to duties lacking
By someone I won't name
Nosey neighbour of the year
Is really put to shame,
She never really misses
All that's going on
Nothing seems to pass her by
When anything goes wrong,
But this time for some reason
I cannot understand
Nosey neighbour of the year
Was head down in the sand,
She missed an opportunity
A golden one at that
To catch a something happening
Right outside her flat,
Arriving in the daytime
The crime was very fast
Lifted from the garden
The thief soon gone and past,
How could the nosey neighbour
Miss the perfect chance
To carry out her duty
With just a single glance,
I think she might be slipping
So I won't tell you her name
The nosey neighbour of the year
Should hang her head in shame!

65. WALKIES BERTIE

Mud, mud wonderful mud
I can get dirty
Just like a dog should,
I can go places
A dog shouldn't go
Finding the mud hidden below!
Wet, wet smelly and rank
Up to my belly
Is just where I sank,
I can find water
Wherever we go
Dirty and smelly above and below!
Dirt, filth anything more
I like to get messy
And roll on the floor
I can do things
A dog shouldn't do
My daddy is daft and hasn't a clue!
Mud, mud dirty old mud
All over my paws
When I ran through the wood
Back to the house
All smelly and wet
I wonder how dirty can I try to get?

66. DREAMS

When you fall asleep and dream
Do you dream of me?
Do you dream of what is past
Or what is yet to be?
Are you sleeping soundly now
Resting in your bed
Or are you feeling restless
With dreams inside your head?
Do you dream in black and white
Or colours bright and new?
Are you in your dreams alone
Or is someone with you?
Are you happy in your dreams
Perhaps you're feeling sad
Do you know what time it is
And all the times you've had
When you close your eyes and dream
How long do you dream?
And when you wake – remember
And wonder what they mean.

67. ANSWER ME THAT

Why can't we appreciate
The setting of the sun?
And why don't we appreciate
A flower till it's gone?
We never seem to notice
The seasons as they change
We seldom seem to hold on to
The love within our range
Why can't we appreciate
The leaves as they change hue?
And why don't we appreciate
An early morning dew?
We never seem to have the time
To stop for just a while
Appreciate the little things
When seen can raise a smile
Why can't we appreciate?
Why can't we take time?
Why can't someone answer
The reason to my rhyme?

68. PRAY SILENCE FOR THE TOAST

Here's to friends
And days gone by,
Things that used to be,
Here's to happy memories,
Friends to you and me.
Let's remember
Not forget,
Those who came along,
Helping us through hard times
Making us feel strong.
Here's to those
Who mean the most,
No stranger to the heart,
Here's to what the future brings
And may we never part.

69. HEROES

In days of old our knights were bold
Not running round a track,
Nor swimming in a swimming pool
There's something they now lack.
In days of old so I've been told
Our heroes were real men,
Who fought for King and country
But that was way back then.
Those days of old are now grown cold
Our knights don't really shine,
Their armour made from lycra now
It really seems a crime.
Those knights of old who once were bold
Their bravery now lost
Replaced by heroes on the field
Playing at what cost?
In days of old our knights once bold
Risking life and limb
Replaced by modern heroes
Whose antics are quite dim.

70. JUST THE SAME ?

Different people,
Different places,
Different smiles
On different faces.
Different joys,
Different tears,
Different worries,
Different fears,
Different thoughts,
Different ways,
Different times,
And different days,
Our differences may not be small,
We're not so different after all.

71. HOPES AND DREAMS

Way back then when I was small
My hopes and dreams seemed very tall,
Hard to climb to, hard to reach
Some like driftwood on a beach,
Some like stars up in the sky
Always there, but far too high.
Things to do and things to be
Places I would go and see,
Travel near or travel far
By plane, train or motor car.
In my head my dreams I see
Some become reality
And some remain just like before
Until I dream my dreams no more.

72. BEFORE, GOODBYE.

I reached the age of eighteen
And wondered who am I?
And where is it I'm going?
Before my time to die.
I looked back on my history
My childhood now was gone
Looking to my future
Would that be very long?
I left behind my schooldays
Summers spent at play
Winters spent in darkness
At the end of every day.
Time to put away the toys
And every comic book
Put away my innocence
Without a backwards look.
And yet as nineteen years approached
Something seemed to say
I might not have those things around
They're not that far away.
As my twenties rolled along
Things began to change
People came into my life
And something felt quite strange.
I met my lifelong partner
Who helped me to forget
Only for a short while
The time before we met.
And as my thirties came around
I still felt young at heart
Some days I would remember
My time back at the start

I'd think back to my innocence
The time I was a youth
Wished that I could go back there
But this was now the truth
Those days were now my history
A fact I had to face
Look towards my future
Accept it with a grace
Happily we rolled along
Forty swept right in
My forties really seemed to end
Before they could begin
And still I looked back on my past
And wished that we were there
Innocent and younger
Without a single care
And now that I've hit fifties
The time just seems to fly
I know I'll never go back
So I'll say a last goodbye.

73. AN OLD HAT AND AN OVERCOAT

The cupboard door was locked and jammed
Sealed well up by rust
But hanging there and long forgot
Gathering up the dust
An old hat and an overcoat
Left there many years
The first time that I saw it
I shed a couple tears.

At first I couldn't find a key
I searched around the place
Inside drawers on top of shelves
In every tiny space
The old hat and the overcoat
Had been there for so long
Forgotten all about them
I'd thought those things were gone.

They brought back many memories
Some of them were sad
But as I thought about them
I soon felt very glad
An old hat and an overcoat
That you used to wear
Brought back happy memories
Of times we used to share.

74. HAPPY TOO ?

If the rain stops falling
Then I'll take you out
Until then you'll have to wait
Please don't make me shout
I've told you once, I'll say again
I'm not getting wet
No matter how you look at me
How sad your eyes may get
Do not look so pleadingly
I simply will not look
You can sit there quietly
While I read my book
Do not raise your paw to me
Here we will remain
I am staying warm and dry
As long as there is rain
Well now you've got your own way
And I am soaked right through
How can you be soaking wet
Yet look so happy too?

75. MISTAKEN IDENTITY

You look a different way today
Have you changed your hair?
A different shade of lipstick?
I hate to stand and stare.
A different kind of make-up?
I cannot quite explain
You look a little different
No –
Let me try again!
Have you lost some weight dear?
Or wearing different clothes?
It isn't that you're wearing
That huge ring through your nose!
I know you're looking different
Please-
Don't tell me yet
WHAT-
You mean to tell me
We have never met!

www.ingramcontent.com/pod-product-compliance
Lightning Source LLC
Chambersburg PA
CBHW061459040426
42450CB00008B/1423